# How To Convince Your Parents You Can...

# Care For A Pet Mouse

Amie Jane Leavitt

*Mitchell Lane*
PUBLISHERS

P.O. Box 196
Hockessin, Delaware 19707
Visit us on the web: www.mitchelllane.com
Comments? email us: mitchelllane@mitchelllane.com

Printing        1     2     3     4     5     6     7     8     9

**A Robbie Reader/How to Convince Your Parents You Can...**

Care for a Pet Chameleon
Care for a Pet Chimpanzee
**Care for a Pet Mouse**
Care for a Pet Snake
Care for a Pet Tarantula

Library of Congress Cataloging-in-Publication Data

Leavitt, Amie Jane.
  Care for a pet mouse / by Amie Jane Leavitt.
     p. cm. — (A Robbie reader)
  Includes bibliographical references and index.
  ISBN-13: 978-1-58415-606-2 (library bound)
  1. Mice as pets—Juvenile literature. I. Title.
  SF459.M5L43 2007
  636.935'3—dc22
                                        2007000820

ABOUT THE AUTHOR: Amie Jane Leavitt, an accomplished author and photographer, was surprised to discover how much she enjoyed writing and researching this particular book. Throughout her life, she has always been terrified of mice. Yet, after completing this book, she can now see why people love having these animals as pets. She actually thinks the animals aren't too bad now herself. Amie graduated from Brigham Young University as an education major and since then has taught all subjects and grade levels in both private and public schools. As an author, she has written numerous books, games, puzzles, and articles for kids and adults. She has also worked as a travel writer and photographer for online and print media and as a consultant, writer, and editor for various educational publishing and assessment companies. Amie has many hobbies, but above all she is an adventurer who loves to travel the globe in search of interesting story ideas and beautiful places to capture on film.

PHOTO CREDITS: All photographs © 2008 JupiterImages Corporation.

# TABLE OF CONTENTS

Words in **bold** type can be found in the glossary.

A mouse uses its tiny paws to climb to the top of its toy wheel. Mice are fun to watch when they play.

1

# A PET TO FIT IN YOUR POCKET

What's small, furry, and very cuddly? A mouse, of course. When many people think of getting a pet, they think about puppies and kittens—but those aren't the only kinds of pets to own. Some people like having **unique** (yoo-NEEK) pets. They want to have something different than what their friends have. That's one reason many people like owning mice.

What is so nice about mice? First, these pets are very small. They can sit in the palm of your hand. They can even hide in your shirt pocket. How many pets can do that? Not many. Mice are happy living in small spaces. For their house, they only need a small cage. This makes it very workable if you don't have much room in your house for a pet.

Another good thing about mice is that they keep themselves very clean. You have to give your dog a bath to keep it clean—but not a mouse. It cleans

itself all the time. These animals know how to bathe themselves from the time they are babies. Even before a baby mouse has opened its eyes, it is already cleaning its skin with its tongue.

Have you asked for a pet but your parents have said pets are too expensive? If so, you might want to ask them for a mouse. Mice are very cheap to buy. Their cages do not cost a lot, either. And you will not have to spend a lot of money on food for this pet. Mice eat very little each day.

Do you want a pet that you can train to do tricks? There's no need to get a dog for that. A mouse can do tricks too! Mice are very smart. You can train them to run through mazes and climb ladders. You can teach them to walk up your arm and sit on your shoulder. You can even train them to jump through hoops. If you really spend some time with it, your pet mouse will sit and beg for its food like a dog.

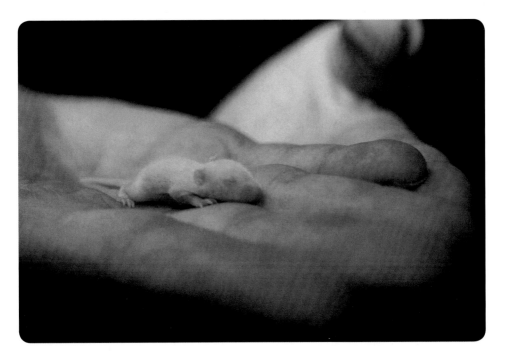

When born, mice are barely the size of an adult human's thumb. Just like dogs and cats, baby mice, or "pinkies," are born with their eyes sealed closed. Their eyes will open when they are about ten days old.

Mice are some of the best pets for kids. Why? One reason is that they sleep during the day and play at night. So while you are in school, your pet will be resting. When you come home, it will be ready to play with you. How great is that? Do you think you want to get a mouse of your own? If so, you'll want to read the rest of this book to learn all about this animal.

Mice in the wild use leaves and twigs to build their nests. They also use these materials to hide from predators. Mice in the wild are usually brown or gray, which helps them blend in with their environment.

**Chapter Two** 2

## MICE IN THE WILD

Mice are **mammals** (MAA-muls). Mammals are animals that are covered with hair. They have a four-chambered heart. The mothers produce milk in their body, which they feed to their babies. Humans are a type of mammal too.

Mice are a type of mammal called **rodents** (ROH-dunts). Other kinds of rodents are rats, squirrels, and beavers. Rodents have many things in common. One is that they have sharp, long front teeth called **incisors** (in-SY-zers).

Humans have incisors too. These are the four lower and four upper front teeth in your mouth. The incisors of rodents are not like the teeth in people. Human teeth grow to a certain size, then stop. The teeth of rodents keep growing all the time. They would grow ten or twenty feet long if they could! That is why rodents like to chew on things.

Chewing helps them wear down their front teeth so that they don't get too long. Keeping their teeth short is very important. If their teeth get too long, they won't be able to eat.

Most scientists agree that mice first lived in Asia. They came to Europe when people traded goods with one another. The mice would hop inside bags of grain and other food, then get carried to new places. They would also sneak aboard ships. When the ships would land, the mice would scurry off to their new homes. Now mice live just about everywhere on earth.

Mice are most often found in forests and grasslands, often near humans. In winter, they will move into people's houses. They live in groups called **colonies** (CAH-luh-nees). Usually, a colony has just one male mouse and many other female mice and their young. They build nests out of grass and wood. Some mice build their nests aboveground. Other

Wild mice dig tunnels for their homes. They will sometimes build their tunnels under barns or houses, where they can find plenty of food.

types dig tunnels. They will store food in one tunnel but use a different tunnel for eating. Mice will dig separate tunnels to use for sleeping. And they'll use one tunnel as their bathroom. These tunnels are like rooms in a house.

Mice are very small animals. Most types grow only as long as three inches. They are also very light. They may weigh only one ounce or less.

Mice live in areas with lots of plants, and their favorite foods grow in the ground. They eat seeds, grains, fruits, and vegetables. Sometimes they'll also eat worms and insects. There are some mice that will even eat other mice. Mice are **omnivores** (OM-nih-vors), which means they will eat both plants and animals.

In the wild, mice usually live only two years. Since they don't live very long, they start having babies at a very young age. A female mouse can start having babies when she is only six weeks old. Mice also have a lot of babies.

House mice can have babies every ten weeks. Each time, the mother mouse can have as many as ten mice. That means that in a year, one mouse could have 50 babies. This is one reason it's so important to keep mice out of your house. And no wonder there are so many mice in the wild.

Mice have poor eyesight. To make up for that, their senses of smell, touch, and hearing are really good.

A mouse's sense of smell is very important. It helps the animal find food and tells it when a **predator** (PREH-dih-ter) is coming. It also helps mice find each other to mate.

Mice can hear **ultrasonic** (ul-truh-SAH-nik) sounds—sounds that are out of the range of human hearing. Mice make these sounds when they want to talk to each other.

Mother mice are very protective of their young. They clean and feed their tiny babies, and they keep them safe from harm. The babies will be hairless for about six days.

Have you ever noticed the whiskers on mice? All rodents have them. These whiskers can sometimes be as long as the mouse's whole body. Mice use their whiskers to help them "see." Whiskers can feel air movement, and they can brush against things. Using their whiskers, mice know where they are going just by feeling the world around them.

A pile of mice waiting to be adopted. There are many things to think about when choosing your new pet. One of them is deciding among the variety of colors.

## CHOOSING A PET MOUSE

Before you buy your pet mouse, there are a number of things you should know. First, how can you tell if your pet is healthy? You can look for many clues.

What does the mouse's fur look like? Is it shiny and clean, or is it dull and dirty? A healthy mouse will clean itself all the time, so don't buy a dirty one!

Look at the eyes, mouth, and ears of the mouse. Is there liquid coming out of them? Are there little sores near the ears? If so, the mouse is probably very sick. Leave this one at the pet store.

Mice also like to run around their cages and play. If a mouse is sitting in the corner and not moving around, it could just be tired—or it could be very sick. It's better to choose a mouse that is playing rather than one that is hunched in the corner.

Many people think it is best to buy mice from private **breeders** (BREE-ders) instead of from a pet

Mice that are bred for sale are less likely than wild mice to have diseases.

store. Why? Private breeders will usually take very good care of their pets. They will be able to show you the parents. Their mice are usually stronger and healthier than mice sold at a pet store.

   If you do decide to buy a mouse at a pet store, you should choose the store carefully. Make sure the pet store is clean. If they take care of their store, they probably take care of their animals. Ask the pet store owner lots of questions. If they don't know anything about mice, then they probably don't take

**funFACTS**

Mice have 18 toes. They have five on each back foot and four on each front foot.

care of them very well either.

It is definitely not a good idea to catch a mouse from the wild and keep it as your pet. Even if the mouse has slipped into your house, you should not catch it and keep it. Keeping wild animals as pets is never a good idea. There are many reasons for this. One is that wild animals carry diseases. Mice can carry one of the deadliest diseases, the hantavirus. It is spread to humans when they breathe the dust from a rodent's dried droppings. If a person gets this disease, it is very hard to cure. If you want a mouse as a pet, it is better to buy one from a breeder or from a pet store than to capture one on your own.

There are many different colors of mice. In the wild, they are usually only gray or brown, sometimes with a lighter-colored belly. This coloring helps hide the mouse from predators. Pet mice can be very different. They have been bred to be white, black, blue, red, tan, and silver. You can even find some

Mice love to play. Choose a mouse that is running and climbing in its cage. This is one way to tell whether a mouse is healthy.

that have fur with spots and other patterns. Look around until you find the pet mouse that is perfect for you.

    After you choose your mouse, you need to buy it a home. Wire cages are the best, as long as the bottom is not made of wire. If it is, you should cover it with wood chips. Mice will hurt their feet if they walk across this wire for very long.

    Mice like to play, so look for toys you can put in their house for them. These don't have to be anything fancy. Mice are even happy playing with

empty toilet paper rolls. Other things that mice find fun are wheels, tissues, clay flowerpots, ladders, and cotton ropes.

A mouse will get lonely if it doesn't have a friend to play with. You can play with your mouse every night, or you might want to think about getting more than one mouse. It's better if you get two or even three female mice, though. Males from different litters will fight with each other, and if you mix a male with a female, they will make too many babies. Some pet owners say it's best if you don't get male mice at all. Why? The males are a little stinkier than the females. However, if you clean the cage out often, then it doesn't matter which kind you get.

Another thing to get for the cage is wood chips and hay or bedding that is made for mice. The mouse will use the hay to make a nest for sleeping. The wood chips will help the mouse feel like it is living in its natural home, the forest.

Mice are happy with lots of things in their cage. Since mice can jump about twelve inches high, always remember to use a lid. A wire lid is probably the best, because the wire will let in enough air for the mice to breathe. Just be sure it fastens tightly.

## A MOUSE IN THE HOUSE

Having a pet mouse brings a few responsibilities. One task to remember is to clean its cage. You should do this once a week. If you don't, the cage will begin to stink.

When you take your pet mouse out of its cage, put it in another cage or box, as long as it's not made of cardboard. Remember, mice like to chew everything. In no time at all, your mouse could chew through the cardboard and escape. Mice are very hard to catch—they can run as fast as 8 miles an hour— so it's best if you put it in something that it can't get out of.

Be really careful when you take your pet out of its cage. Never pick up your mouse by its tail. You also don't want your mouse to run away.

Once you remove the mouse, you will have to dump all the wood chips and hay from the cage into the trash. Then, clean the cage with soap and water. Once the cage is dry, put in new wood chips and hay or bedding. Your mouse will love having its home cleaned every week.

One thing that is important to remember is to keep your mouse's cage in a safe place. Do not put it near other animals that might hurt it, like cats or dogs. And you'll want to keep it out of direct sunlight. A mouse is covered in fur, and the sunlight will make the cage way too hot. Just imagine if you were wearing a fur coat and sitting in a very hot room and couldn't get out. You should always think of these kinds of things when you have a pet.

It doesn't cost much to buy food for mice. They like to eat rolled oats, carrots, lettuce, cabbage, apples, and potatoes. They'll even eat leftover rice and pasta from your dinner. In the summer, giving a mouse dandelion flowers is a special treat. And every once in a while, you can feed it sunflower seeds.

Mice like to eat many different kinds of food. A selection of snacks—such as a mixture of grain, rice, seeds, and corn—is something your pet mouse will really love.

Don't do so very often, since these are very high in fat and could make your mouse gain too much weight. Remember to take any old food out of the cage once a day. Your mouse could get sick if it eats something that is rotten.

Another thing your mouse must have is water. Buy a special container from the pet store that will let the water drip out slowly. These containers keep the water fresh— and they'll keep your mouse safe from falling into an open container and drowning.

You will find that if you follow these simple instructions, your mouse will hardly ever get sick. If it does, you should take it to a **veterinarian** (veh-truh-NAYR-ee-un).

It is a good idea to play with your mouse, but a mouse is fast, so don't let it run out of its cage or you might not be able to find it again. At first, your

## funFACTS

Mice will use one corner of their cage as their toilet. They will not go to the bathroom anywhere else in the cage.

mouse might be afraid of you, and it may not want to play with you. It may not know that you are its kind owner. It may think that you are a predator and will hurt it. Just take it slow. Let your mouse get to know you over time. Soon, it will love you and want to play with you every day.

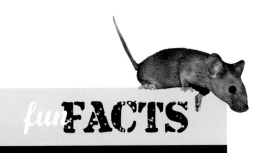

If you are very careful, you can feed your pet mouse right out of your hand. These mice are slurping up some rich, fresh cream.

A mouse runs on its wheel just like a person might run on a treadmill. Mice can make the wheel spin so fast that if they stop running and hold on, the wheel will spin them round and round.

# ARE YOU READY FOR A MOUSE?

It's fun having a pet, but it's also something that the whole family has to agree upon. Do your parents want you to have a pet? What do they think about having a mouse in their house?

If they are nervous about getting a pet, there might be certain reasons why. Mice, especially if they come from the wild, carry a variety of diseases.

Your parents might also worry that you will not take care of your new pet. If this happens, they will have to do all the work, and they might not have the time. Maybe they think that a pet will cost too much money. They might even think that you will get tired of the pet and not want it anymore. They may not know much about the animal that you want to get.

You should talk to your parents about these things. You have learned a lot of facts about mice in this book. Maybe you could tell them some of

When you choose items to put in your mouse cage, be sure they are made of safe, healthy materials. Use untreated wood chips or fresh timothy hay for the floor. Wooden and cardboard toys should not be painted or stained.

the things you have learned. This might help them understand that mice are fun animals to have in the house. You could also make sure your parents know that you are serious about wanting a pet. You could promise them that you will be responsible. You will take care of the pet, and they won't have to worry. Of course, you can only promise these things if you really plan to do them. You have to make sure in your own mind that you really want to be a pet owner before you get your pet.

Owning a pet is a big responsibility. It can be a lot of fun, but it is also something that you have to think about every day. If your parents think you are ready for a pet, then maybe you will decide to get a pet mouse. They're cute, cuddly, and a lot of fun. The two of you could be very happy together!

## Books and Articles

Arenofsky, Janice. "Nice Mice." *Jack & Jill Magazine.* October 1, 2002.

Henrie, Fiona. *Mice and Rats.* London: Franklin Watts, 1980.

"Pet Mice-Nice?" *Ranger Rick.* November 2003.

Sjonger, Rebecca. *Mice (Pet Care, 5).* New York: Crabtree Publishing Company, 2004.

Wexler, Jerome. *Pet Mice.* Niles, Illinois: Albert Whitman & Company, 1989.

## Works Consulted

Hirschhorn, Howard. *Guide to Owning a Mouse.* Neptune City, New Jersey: T.F.H. Publications, 2003.

Shulman, Stephanie. *The Mouse: An Owner's Guide to a Happy Healthy Pet.* New York: Howell Book House, 2000.

Vanderlip, Sharon. Mice: *A Complete Pet Owner's Manual.* New York: Barron's Educational Series, 2001.

Vandivert, Rita. *Understanding Animals as Pets.* New York: Frederick Warne & Company, 1975.

Weber, William J. *Care of Uncommon Pets.* New York: Henry Holt and Company, 1979.

## Web Addresses

The London and Southern Counties Mouse and Rat Club:
http://www.miceandrats.com

The British Broadcasting Corporation – Pets:
http://www.bbc.co.uk/cbbc/wild/pets/mouse.shtml

The Humane Society of the United States:
http://www.hsus.org/animals_in_research/species_used_in_research/mouse.html

Pet Facts – Mice:
http://www.abc.net.au/creaturefeatures/facts/mice.htm

**breeder** (BREE-der)—a person who mates animals so that the young can be sold to other people.

**colonies** (CAH-luh-nees)—groups of animals or plants that live together in the same place.

**incisors** (in-SY-zers)—the sharp teeth in the front of the mouth that are used for cutting.

**mammals** (MAA-muls)—animals that have hair, feed their babies milk, and have a heart with four chambers.

**omnivores** (OM-nih-vors)—animals that eat both plants and other animals.

**predator** (PREH-dih-ter)—an animal that hunts other animals for food.

**rodent** (ROH-dunt)—a group of small mammals that have large, chisel-shaped incisors.

**ultrasonic** (ul-truh-SAH-nik)—sounds that are higher than the human ear can hear.

**unique** (yoo-NEEK)—special, different from other things.

**veterinarian** (veh-truh-NAYR-ee-un)—a doctor who takes care of animals.

# INDEX